MEDITATIONS FOR DOGS

PITHY POOCHIE PONDERINGS

PHOTOGRAPHS
BY ANNE HERMAN

Andrews McMeel Publishing

Kansas City

You will do foolish things

but do them

with enthusiasm.

—*Colette*

There is no such thing

as inner peace.

There is only nervousness and death.

—*Fran Lebowitz*

The cure for boredom is curiosity.

There is no cure for curiosity.

—*Ellen Parr*

You were once wild here.

Don't let them tame you!

—*Isadora Duncan*

My bed shall comfort me,
my couch shall ease my complaint.

— *Job 7:13*

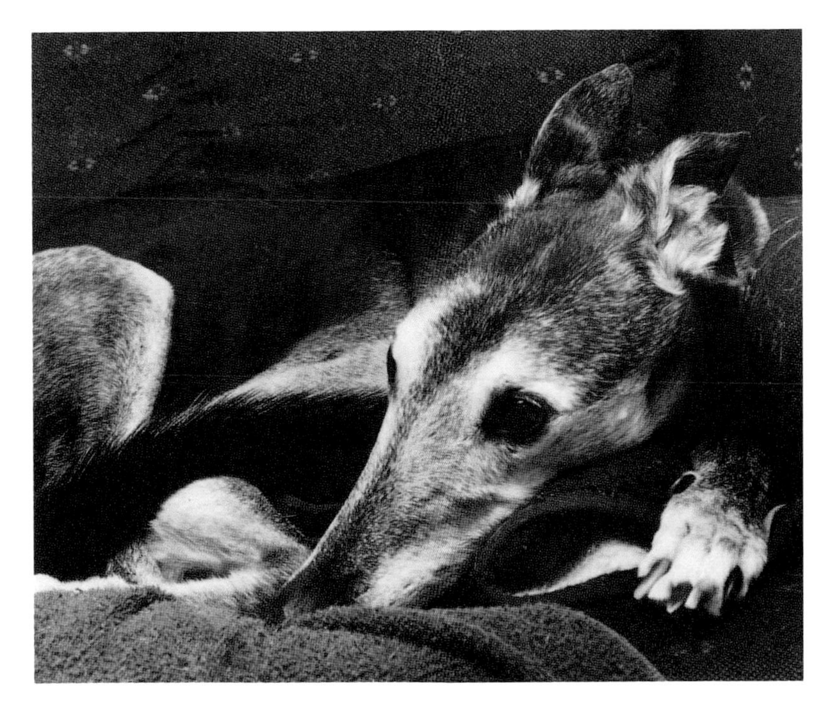

I have found that if you love life,
life will love you back.

—*Arthur Rubinstein*

Eye contact is a humanizing element
in an often impersonal world.

—*Michael Gelb*

Of the thirty-six alternatives,

running away is the best.

—*Chinese proverb*

A heart set on love
will not do wrong.

—*Confucius*

What'll we do with ourselves this afternoon?

And the day after that,

and the next thirty years?

—F. Scott Fitzgerald

Henceforth I whimper no more,
postpone no more, need nothing . . .
Strong and content I travel the open road.

—*Walt Whitman*

Does the name Pavlov ring a bell?

—*Unknown*

If you don't know where you are going,

you could wind up someplace else.

—*Yogi Berra*

I became insane . . .

with intervals of horrible sanity.

—Edgar Allen Poe

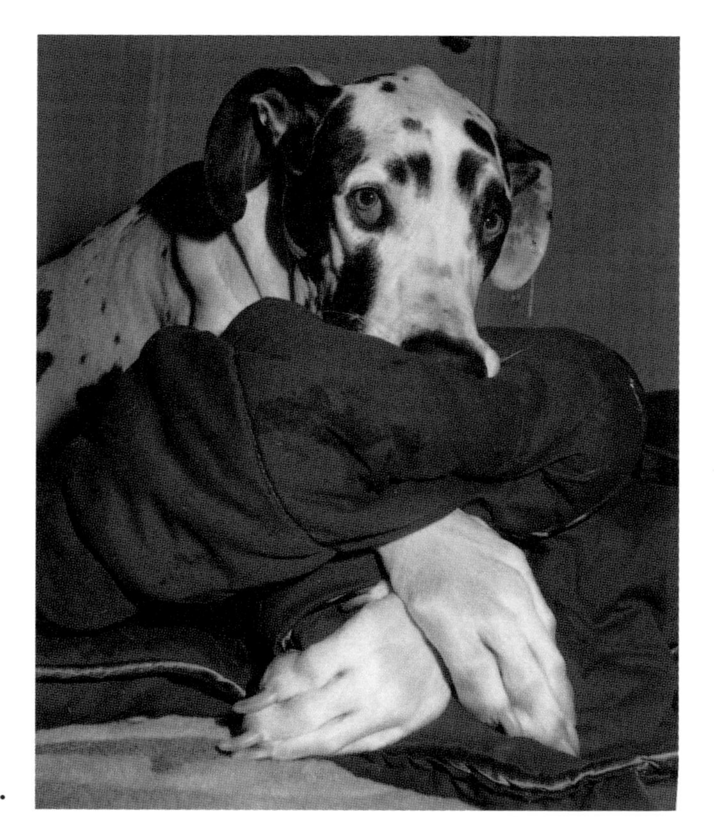

It is easier to be gigantic

than to be beautiful.

—Friedrich Wilhelm Nietzsche

He that is giddy
thinks the world turns round.

—*William Shakespeare*

Some mornings
it just doesn't seem worth it
to gnaw through the leather straps.

—*Emo Philips*

Think it no shame

to be helped.

—*Marcus Aurelius*

So little time

and so little to do.

—*Oscar Levant*

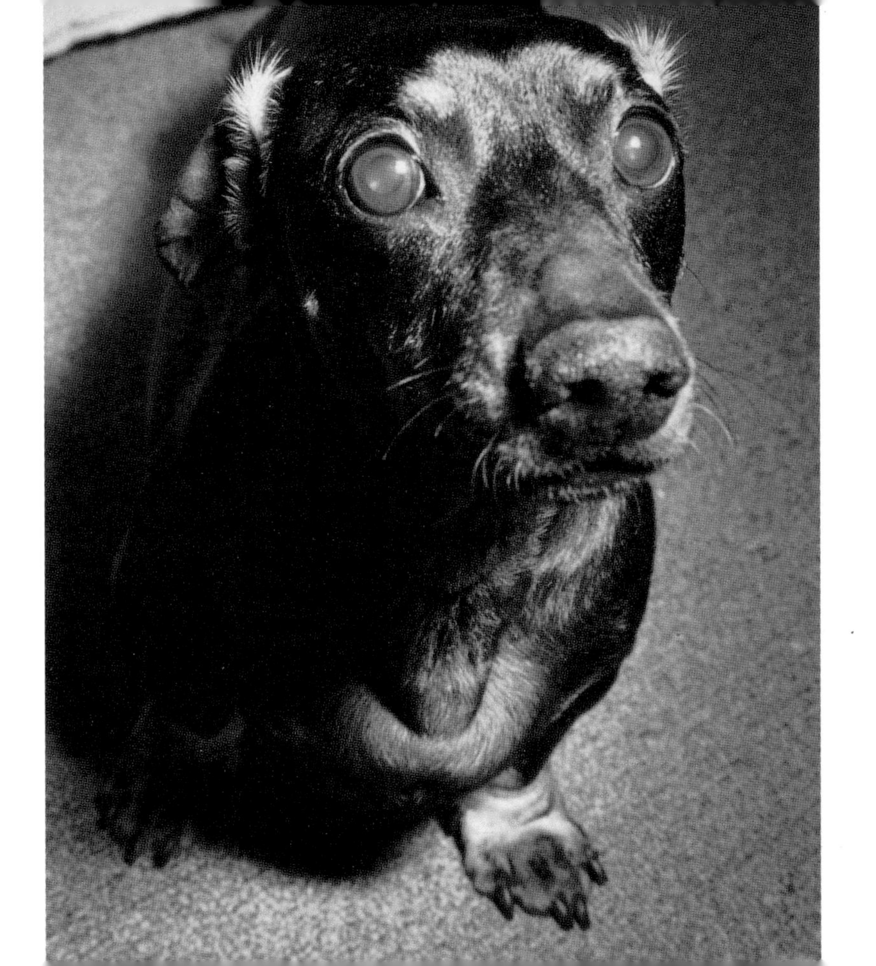

It is hard to fight an enemy
who has outposts in your head.

—*Sally Kempton*

If it were not for guests,

all houses would be graves.

—Kahlil Gibran

Bathe twice a day to be really clean,

once a day to be passably clean,

once a week to avoid being a public menace.

—*Anthony Burgess*

Thy nose is as the tower of Lebanon
which looketh toward Damascus.

—*Song of Sol. 7:4*

Look twice before you leap.

—*Charlotte Brontë*

A door is what a dog

is perpetually on the wrong side of.

—*Ogden Nash*

Vex not thy spirit
at the course of things.

—*Marcus Aurelius*

If you are all wrapped up in yourself,

you are overdressed.

—*Kate Halverson*

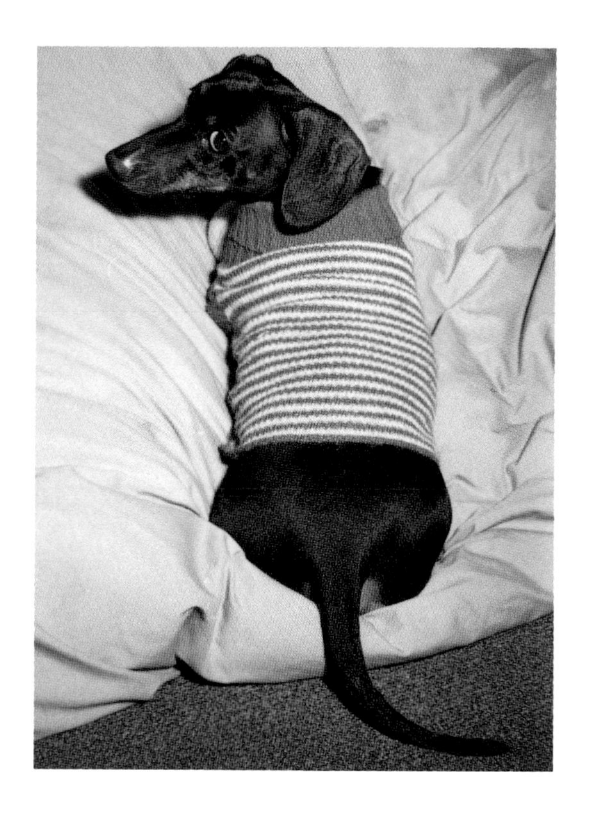

Work is much more fun
than fun.

—Noël Coward

Tell me the company you keep,
and I will tell you who you are.

—Proverb

You are only as good
as your last haircut.

—*Susan Lee*

You know what charm is:

a way of getting the answer yes

without having asked any clear questions.

—Albert Camus

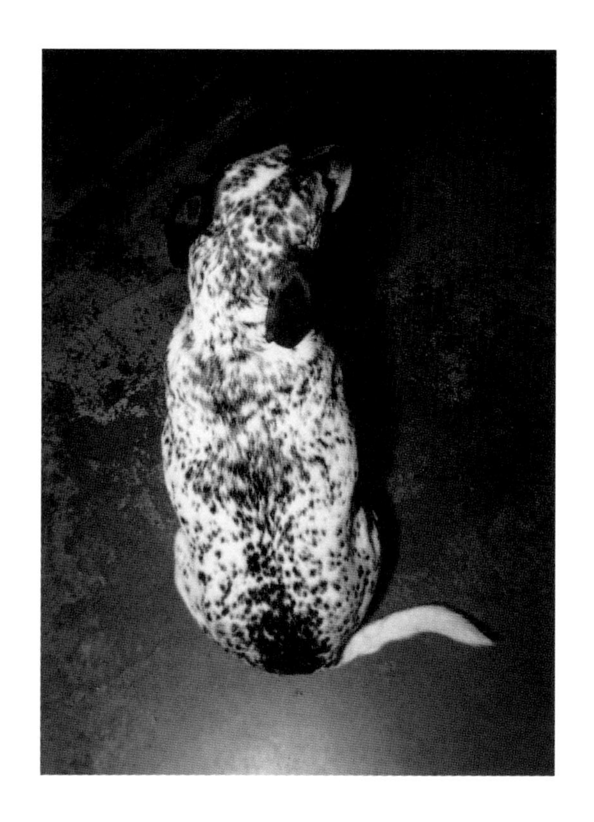

It takes a lot of time to become a genius.
You have to sit around doing nothing,
really doing nothing.

—Gertrude Stein

Seriousness is the only refuge
of the shallow.

—*Oscar Wilde*

What is this life if,

full of care,

we have not time to stand and stare?

—*W. H. Davies*

Who contains himself

goes seldom wrong.

—*Confucius*

I don't care where I sit

as long as I get fed.

—*Calvin Trillin*

If we keep an open mind,
too much is likely to fall into it.

—*Natalie Clifford Barney*

My life has been one long descent
into respectability.

—*Mandy Rice-Davies*

The world is round
and the place which may seem like the end
may also be the beginning.

—*Ivy Baker Priest*

 For information, write Andrews McMeel Publishing, an Andrews McMeel Universal company, 4520 Main Street, Kansas City, Missouri 64111.

ISBN: 0-7407-1915-7

Library of Congress Catalog Card Number: 2001086421